What You Need to Know About

The Person

You Want to Become

Aaron Zigler

Quantity sales special discounts are available on quantity purchases by corporations, associations, and others. For details, contact the publisher at the address above.

Orders by U.S. trade bookstores and wholesalers. Email info@BeyondPublishing.net

The Beyond Publishing Speakers Bureau can bring authors to your live event. For more information or to book an event contact the Beyond Publishing Speakers Bureau speak@BeyondPublishing.net

The Author can be reached directly at BeyondPublishing.net

Manufactured and printed in the United States of America distributed globally by BeyondPublishing.net

BEYOND
PUBLISHING

New York | Los Angeles | London | Sydney

ISBN Hardcover: 978-1-637922-31-6

ISBN Softcover: 978-1-637922-35-4

TABLE OF CONTENTS

CHAPTER 1

Make Your Bed

Waking up every morning, we determine how our day is going to go. We set the tone, or the mood of the day, with our feelings- maybe I reach straight for the phone, feeling anxious and distracted. Perhaps I race out of bed, in a hurry to get going on the list of things I need to do. It is easy to forget the basics, all of the things that keep my life from falling into chaos. I need to take care of myself, I need to stay grounded and organized. Some people have morning meditation practices, some people make a gratitude list in their heads- for me, I do something much simpler, and I would argue, more rewarding - I make my bed.

Making my bed is giving a gift to my older self. Granted, a day older, but still, older. The me I am becoming, the me I am meant to be. I see that person, and I want to give them the pleasure of a nicely made bed. In this way, no matter what I do in my day, what I have to deal with, how distracted I get, I know that I am coming back to the gift of a made bed at the end of the day.

Beyond the creature comforts of a nicely made bed, there is a virtue and discipline in doing something that you probably don't want to do - and having that be the first thing you do - it makes all the other things you will encounter in your day somehow easier. Making my bed is one of the first things my parents taught me, they were wise to teach me to get comfortable doing things that are at first uncomfortable. They were also wise to show me that often momentary discomfort pays off big time with the reward of later comfort, a comfort that far outweighs the discomfort it took to get there- this is a lesson for businesses, relationships, going through hell, and hell, even going through life.

We have to develop tenacity in this life. We have to learn how to get where we want to go. We have to invite that in. If you work hard every day, a clean and well made bed becomes the baseline out of which you can recharge and operate. A well made bed says that though my external life may look like madness, my internal world is solid, stable, and consistent. This is the kind of attitude that reaps major rewards. Though it is easy to rush in the morning toward the first task, our first task ought to be investing in our future self - in the person we want to become - and the easiest way to do that is by giving the gift of a clean bed.

We are always tasked with doing things that we may not like to do - paying taxes, jury duty, finishing a difficult course in school - these are all things that keep us tethered to society and others - making our bed keeps us tethered to ourselves.

Let me tell you a story about when my bed wasn't made: I was working a job that I hated. Every morning, I would wake up and my first feeling was one of apathy. I hated even existing. My bed came to symbolize that. I had no regard for the person who would drive home from work every day, so I didn't care whether or not they had the pleasure of a clean bed, of a meaningful and organized life. We live in metaphors, and the world we create around us does determine how we feel. As if out of the blue, one morning I decided to make my bed. Coming home that night, I had a visceral sense of what it felt like to be cared for, and more importantly, to care for myself. I had a glimmer again of my value and potential.

Yes, it may seem far fetched that all of this came from simply making my bed.

However, sometimes the simplest, easiest gestures are simple and easy for a reason, and the reason we avoid them speaks to the resistance we have toward becoming the person we are meant to be.

Make your bed, see what happens, see how it feels - at the very least, you will look forward to coming home every day, or you will be surprised by the mindfulness and foresight of your younger self - a feeling that will follow you into all the arenas of your life.

CHAPTER 2

Call a Loved One

This exercise is aimed at making you realize all that you need to do to keep those close who love you and who you love back. Oftentimes, we take for granted those relationships that are nearest to us. Other times, we are paired up with someone- a close relative, an old childhood friend - and we are forced to be close with someone we don't really like. I am sure you can think of someone who fits that description. Now - consider all you have done to support a relationship that is inevitable. Our lives can change when we embrace that which is difficult for us emotionally to do. A great first step is to reach out to someone we are paired with for better or for worse, and to extend to them a gesture of openness and receptivity.

Think about a friend who has always been there for you - somehow, you always hug and make up, no matter what happens. These are the kinds of friendships that keep our lives afloat. This is what is possible when we know that the person will be with us no matter what, through thick and thin. So why not make a first effort now into a relationship that you know will last - because of the nature of that relationship - and express some gratitude for something between the two of you. This gets to a lesson that can help you navigate in situations that are more apparently difficult. When you find yourself working with colleagues who are frustrating, it is easy to lash out at them, because something about the relationship seems temporary or transactional. However, when you take a step back and approach it as if it were one of the aforementioned relationships, much can open up for you.

Being in sales, friendliness and congeniality were essential parts of finding a shared goal between me and the person on the other end of the sale. These were not for show, these were the tools I used to do my job. We are always selling our best self, or trying to - but a first step is sharing the kind of friendliness and congeniality that is most often absent where we feel we need it least- in our most stable and solid relationships. By consciously applying it there, it spills out into the rest of our life and world.

An example from my life - for me, it is my parents. I know that I am blessed with loving parents. There is almost nothing in this world that I could do and that they wouldn't forgive. Because of this, my parents are often the ones who receive the blunt end of my nonsense.

With them, I can be my worst self more often than with any other person, because I feel that their love is secure. This can wear at our relationship, it can affect my ability to feel loved and supported. This, of course, is a misunderstanding. Some people have relationships with parents that are tragically broken beyond repair, but everyone has someone who is a bright star in their life, an essential part of their support system. Think for a minute how you treat that person compared to other people? When you have nothing to gain from them, do you take the relationship more for granted? I know I can. I also know that by consciously applying friendliness and gratitude to those relationships, it spills out into the rest of my life.

We need to do our best to become the person that we want to be. That starts with recognizing the relationships we fail to nurture -- which more often than not are the relationships closest to us --and nurture them.

CHAPTER 3

Younger Self Letter

How much of our own life do we have control over? Answer: none of it when we aren't aware of what has control over us. We need to look back into the shadowy history of our lives and pull out the things that were there, which affected us greatly, and which we had no control over at the time. The practice of writing a letter to your younger self can aid tremendously in making this kind of perspective possible. This perspective unlocks your future.

By handing your earlier self a message from your older self, you set in motion a process of recognition and healing, reconciliation with the truth that you somehow survived all the attacks and impossible situations. Perhaps it will offer you some closure on a younger form of yourself, and help solidify the new you. It will show you how you have grown and changed, and unlock the possibility of more growth and change in the direction you wish to go.

I wanted to tell my younger self about addiction. All people are susceptible to addictions. For some it is money, others fame, sadly for many it is drugs and alcohol. For me, it was love. I did so many dumb things, and suffered so many emotions. All because I wasn't aware I even had a problem that in some ways were outside of my control.

When I became aware that I was a love addict. I was able to assess the situation and move on, I was able to grow and develop into the person I wanted to be. However, writing a letter to my younger self, and letting him know what was going on in my imagination, that so much of his pain and hurt was something he just didn't have control over, this made me feel closure, self forgiveness, and freed up a lot of creative energy to focus on the present moment. I couldn't build what I am building now without that closure, that distance, and that kind of self love.

My mind is greater and my path more free because I have learned to change what I can change and accept that I didn't have full control over my life in the past. My younger self was subject to things that he didn't have the tools or power to change. Writing a letter, even if it is just in your head, thinking about what you would tell your younger self if you met them on the street - and not with a goal of changing them or giving them secrets to success, rather just pointing out that so much of what they are experiencing are due to factors outside of their control - is the first major step in getting control and moving on with your life. [insert illustration of an open road]

Without an eye toward giving your younger self what you lacked then, but toward giving yourself an understanding of your world then - what would you want your younger self to know about the world around them? Is it unnecessarily cruel? Is it full of people who want to use them? Is it plagued by an addiction they don't fully comprehend? Is it a world they are trying to change in ways that aren't true to themselves? A world of false expectations or ideals? In this way, you are realizing so many of the things that were outside of your control, or outside of yourself that caused you to suffer. You are able to transform this into a newfound awareness that brings greater control and freedom in your world today.

CHAPTER 4

Older Self Letter

I was once told "you overestimate what you can do in a year, and you underestimate what you can do in five." The last section was about making peace with your past. This exercise is about imagining your future without any restraint or limitation. We enter into our future every day, in fact, every moment, and we come to know ourselves through this string of little futures. This is a big thought, sure, but if you break it down, all that it shows us is how quickly life moves along. In the words of Ferris Bueller, "Life moves pretty fast, if you don't stop and look around once and a while, you could miss it." Consider this exercise stopping and looking around. [Insert picture of a man thinking].

Wind back five years time. If you would have told me then that I would be writing a book, I wouldn't have believed you. If I had written a letter to myself, saying that I wanted to do all those things in a year, it would not have happened.

If, however, I fast-forwarded to a much older version of myself, and wrote a letter to that person, requesting that they had done many of the things I am trying to do now. What that gesture did was put everything in its proper place and in the right timeline. Having these thoughts on a five year map, I started becoming the person I wanted to be.

By writing a letter, even if only in your mind, to your older self, you articulate the person you want to become - more importantly, you free yourself up from false expectations and timelines. In effect, you give yourself permission to be that person now, and to watch what comes from it.

This is one of the marvelous things about being who you are and becoming the person you are meant to become. It all starts with owning the fact that you are that person, and one way to do that is of course by writing it down, vocalizing it to yourself, or telling a friend. Often though, aspirations are most powerful when they are kept near to you and those close to you. That is why I would recommend writing it in the form of a letter to your older self

Who is that person and what have they become and accomplished? - and tucking it away in a safe space. This serves as your map, and the goals you can build towards.

CHAPTER 5

Talk to Someone New

The world is always waiting to help us become the person we want to be, we just have to stretch out our hand to meet it. So often, we close ourselves off to our ultimate potential by relying more on our own will and drive, and never welcoming the support and guidance-- the opportunity-- others are able to afford us with. So often, a life changing event is as far away as a handshake or a hello. How I came to be writing this book is a fine example of that. I was at a conference, when I was 20, centered around putting purpose to action. How I came to even be at that conference is a story unto itself, but it suffices to say, I wasn't really supposed to be there by any normal metric of the imagination. I found myself, after a full day of lectures and collaboration with much having been learned, feeling ready to give back to this conference in a pure and uncomplicated way.

As I was walking out for the day, I noticed that there were some people struggling to move heavy tables. I introduced myself and offered them a hand. As we were moving these tables, they mentioned that they were headed to a conference after-party for networking.

Although I wasn't yet 21, I was invited, and once I was there, I naturally started to meet people, which further led to the introduction of others, which in turn led to this book.

My life was changed by reaching out to a stranger, in a spirit of helpfulness and friendliness, and yours could be too. There are countless other stories like it. I know someone who landed their first big Wall Street account by making small talk with someone on the subway, when they were a new broker in New York City, nearly penniless. They didn't come across as desperate, just genuine and interested. Granted, this was the days before everyone on the subway is plugged into headphones, and a little casual chat could help move along the train ride, but opportunities like it are plentiful -- we just have to learn to pay attention and develop the inner trust and vulnerability to reach out.

Let's talk more about steps we can take to develop what we need to reach out to someone new, someone we find interesting. We need to realize that we aren't looking to gain anything from them -- that is the most important first step. Of course, to make that happen, we have to get there internally. No one else is your golden ticket, you are your own golden ticket, and by remembering that, you are able to invite other people to support you on your path of becoming the person you want to be. So try it out, talk to someone new, see how it makes you feel, for all you know, it could lead to the next big thing.

CHAPTER 6

Your Peak Experiences

In Northern California, there are huge cliffs above beautiful lakes and rivers. With the right mindset, it is possible to leap from a cliff, enjoy a long free fall, and feel your body plunge into the depths.

There is something cathartic about taking this kind of risk, and about being this close to the natural world, where animals and plants take risks every day to ensure their survival.

Humans have grown to be different. We need to take risks based on what we love, that makes our choices feel like less of a risk. I love the feeling of flying through the air. I know it is risky, but it is worth it because I love it.

The same advice could be applied to a number of arenas-- relationship, business, maybe even health-- but for the sake of this journey into getting to know the person you want to become, it is your relationship with you that matters. Think about the peak experiences in your life. How can you take those and make a plan about what you want to do in the world and who you want to be? I will share my own story to lead the way.

For me, it wasn't the peak experience of cliff jumping-though that attitude certainly affects how I live my life and run my business- it was rather a certain afternoon in Angel Fire, NM, a small town in the mountains, far away from industry. This experience was just me communing with nature, and with MY nature. I had a vision of creating a difference in the world. I knew this was something that wouldn't just happen by the course of nature, but it would happen by the course of my nature. All I had to do was remember and really own how much I loved this vision for myself, and I started moving in the right direction.

By locating what we love, we also locate our gifts- our gifts are always in service of making what we love a reality or feeding what we love so that it stays vibrant in this world. We are hardwired to do what we love, we just have to open up to it and own it.

So what is your peak experience? Make a list, grab a piece of paper, grab a napkin, grab your phone, think about and jot down what comes to mind. Then take a closer look, what in these peak experiences did you love. Was it working with other people, was it making something others enjoyed? And then dig deeper, what kind of person would be the kind of person that connected with this love everyday, what would their life be like? Once you identify that, you have a start to your roadmap for becoming the person you want to be.

CHAPTER 7

The Perfect Push Up

We live in a culture that encourages us to master multiple domains. This can often lead to being mediocre at multiple practices, rather than masterful at one. The great writer and thinker Malcolm Gladwell suggests that in order to attain mastery of something, we have to put in 10,000 hours of practice. Mastery is a daunting task, therefore, it makes sense that most people would rather merely attain proficiency in multiple arenas. But when we look at our list of peak experiences, and begin to map out the person that we want to become, it becomes clear that in order to become that person we will need to put in work. Put simply, we may have to sacrifice other pursuits, in the pursuit of the person we wish to become.

A metaphor that illustrates this well is the idea from martial arts that one push up, properly done, is far more effective in building strength than a hundred pushups done without sufficient attention. One path requires the discipline of attention to detail, not just repetition. This idea pushes Malcom Gladwell's idea of time in, output realized a bit farther. It is not just putting in the hours, it is also sustaining the attention to the task within those hours. This of course is so much easier to do when we are engaging in something that we love.

When we fall in love with what we are doing, and with who we want to become, it becomes a joy to pay attention to the details of our journey there.

So think about what you love, about the person you want to become. What are the things you need to practice to make that so, and what about those things bring you joy? By focusing on the good in the details, practice becomes an expansive experience, rather than a confining or punitive way of trying to get what you want. When we begin slowly laying the foundation of the person we want to become, it makes room for 10,000 hours worth of building to grow upon it. There is an old adage, "If it ain't broke, don't fix it," the same goes for ourselves. Rather than trying to fix ourselves, we just need to spend time focusing and developing the things we already love, for the joy of that alone will propel us into our best future.

CHAPTER 8

Learn a New Recipe

Do you know the feeling of routine gone wrong? Maybe for breakfast every day you have yogurt and granola, and then one morning it just tastes off. You might be perplexed, because you love this. You have come to believe something about yourself is true, and in the past it has been true, but now something just feels wrong. So often, to use this metaphor, we don't mix up our habits because we are too tepid to learn a new recipe. We constantly need to be guessing and reexamining who we think we are in order to find the person we want to become. This starts not only through finding out what it is we want to become, but by actively trying new things that may at first seem unfamiliar. We have to break out of habits to find what it is we are missing.

We learn more about ourselves, our likes and dislikes, by trying new things. This is really the key to success, to be open enough to try anything, and discerning enough - clear enough on who you are - to know what is for you and what isn't for you. Often, we take ourselves by surprise, convinced we feel one way about something only to learn we have other thoughts at play, once we connect with our deeper and truer selves - once we align with the person we want to become.

In my own life, I think about my journey with Higher Education. I never thought I would go to college. I admired the self-made entrepreneurs like Bill Gates and Steve Jobs, or even Bob Dylan, these visionaries who didn't need to complete a traditional education to realize their dreams.

I had a budding career, dare I say blossoming career, and I hit a wall. To overcome that wall, I didn't think I needed to go back to school. I may have wanted to go back to school, but I had convinced myself that I wasn't that person and could succeed on my own. That did not turn out to be true. Consequently, I had to make a drastic change in my life. For me, what was hardest about going to school wasn't the work, it was the change in who I thought I was. But so often, who you think you are is not the same as the person you really want to become.

Sometimes the steps to freeing up blocked energy can be changing little things in your routine. If you always run a set path, change it up a little bit. If you make yourself the same breakfast every day, add something. Most importantly, if you are always telling yourself the same things about what you can and cannot do, try to break out of those patterns of thinking. Start to tell yourself new and different things about what is possible for you in your life. The new goal for you needs to be not just organizing around what you already think you know about the person you want to become, but also it is equally important that it take shape around the person you might not yet know, the person that also needs to have a place at the table now.

One of the best ways to get to know that person is through innovation in your daily life. So take a minute and think about what you can do. Maybe it is as simple as learning a new recipe, maybe it is as involved as going back to school. But as our parents used to always say when we were given a new food to try, "You don't know until you've tasted it".

CHAPTER 9

Get Angry

While growing up, I would hear stories about families that made fortunes by making other people's lives miserable, or not taking the proper steps to ensure that what they were creating would do minimal harm to others or the environment. Sure, there are a lot of bad rich people, just like there are a lot of bad poor people, there are just a lot of bad people out there, rich and poor. I went through a lot of my life compartmentalizing these people. I never got angry about it because I thought it was never my place. The truth was, I never got angry about it because I didn't want to have to engage seriously with those feelings. Once I let myself get angry about it, I realized that I didn't actually have a lot of solid footing for my anger.

If you cannot be critical of the world, you cannot change it for the better. By being critical, and more importantly, being open to feedback on your criticism, you are given a gift. What is this gift? It is the gift of becoming more self aware, of expanding your thinking and feeling. I learned something powerful in getting critical, something powerful about the person I want to become. I want to be someone who utilizes myself correctly, as a way to give back. By being critical and more importantly being able to listen to myself being critical. I am able to take a step back, see my errors, and learn more about the person I really want to become in it all.

Oftentimes, what we are critical of is a piece of the puzzle, and an important one at that, in the work of realizing the person we want to become. But if we never give ourselves permission to be critical, we will never get there. So go ahead and get angry, just be willing to admit that you were wrong, and notice what might come out of the whole experience. More likely than not, it will be the new you.

CHAPTER 10

Accept Mortality

The Declaration of Independence starts, " We hold these truths to be self-evident, that all men are created equal, that they are endowed by their Creator with certain unalienable Rights, that among these are Life, Liberty and the pursuit of Happiness." These words though were written in the midst of a time unlike anything we have seen in our lifetimes, in the United States. These words had in them a sense of our collective mortality, and because of that, of the preciousness of life and the need to preserve that life at any and all costs. For me, my journey of coming to accept my death, and accept that death is a thing that happens, that it is as natural as life itself, is a journey I am still on. I would be lying to say I am already there. But the strides I have made in that direction are hugely beneficial in unlocking my ability to actualize the person I want to become. For me, my pursuit of happiness is made much more real because of the knocking of death on my door. With the time I have left, I might as well do all I can to be happy.

There is the old expression I am sure you have heard, "Carpe Diem" or seize the day. A more literal translation of the expression, from what I've learned, would be to "pluck the day". I like to think about these two different words, seize and pluck, and how much they could be a response to the way we feel about death. Some people smarter than me would say that how we feel about death affects how we live our life. For me, it was through accepting that I will die that I was able to give myself permission to pursue happiness. This was a breakthrough for me, because I could accept how I wanted to live.

I lived my life from a young age ignoring my fear of death. I was in denial about it.

Gradually, I moved from denial to acceptance, and then where I am now, from acceptance to actualization. My fear of death, especially death at a young age, wasn't conquered, but it was recognized. Only after recognizing it for what it is was I able to really start living life on my own terms. I thought about the authors of the Declaration of Independence, and my own pursuit of happiness, grateful that I live in a country where my death can be made easier by a life lived in the way I wanted. So now, if something doesn't make me happy, I change it. And if something does make me happy, I go after it.

Death is a part of life, a troubling and upsetting part of life. We will all experience it, and all experience loved ones departing too. I know for me, when someone I love passes on, the feeling I always have is one of them encouraging me to really love the life I want, and to go and live it. One of the best ways we can honor the forefathers of democracy, and those of our ancestors who have sacrificed so much to give us the safety and security we desire, is by truly finding the person we wish to become, the source of our happiness, and then doing it.

CHAPTER 11

Reflect On Failures

Often we blame others rather than taking personal responsibility ourselves. But here is the thing, there isn't a single situation where you aren't responsible for at least 10 percent of it, besides of course being born. Taking the blame off others isn't just a weight off your shoulders, it helps you learn how much power your choices have. It can help clear things up, often miraculously, by just acknowledging you made a mistake and taking responsibility. Own it. It might be uncomfortable in the moment, you might have missed out on something great, but if you don't own it, you could never have anything like it in the future. Reflecting on failures opens up our futures.

I can think of a story that is a little personal, but I think it illustrates this well. When I was in high school, I got pulled over and there was pot and beer in the car. My heart sank having to make that call to my parents, saying I am in the police station and I need you to come get me. I decided to take the punishment and reflect on my failures, rather than blame anyone or anything else than myself. I understood that I did something wrong, so I have to live through the consequences.

I didn't forget the feeling of doing something wrong. This to me made all the difference. I had taken an action that required a consequence. I chose to accept the consequence. I chose not to try to wiggle my way out of it. I chose to have pot and beer in my car. The cop didn't do that. I did that. I drove with it in my car. Understanding this is simple, but powerful.

This experience in my life reinforced my experience that so many people blame others and don't really look at what they've done. I could have easily blamed that cop for getting me in trouble. I could have blamed others for giving me reasons to want the pot and beer.

No matter how much of someone else's fault I may perceive it to be, I said yes. I said yes to having that stuff in my car. The bottom line is that I chose to accept and take responsibility for what I did, and that had huge benefits for me on the next step of my life.

CHAPTER 12

Forgiveness List

Holding onto resentment of others holds us back in life. What sort of goes hand in hand with taking personal responsibilities for our failures is forgiving others. So often we project onto other people our own failures and then we resent the others, unable or unwilling to see our role in things. This has to change if we want to take massive steps forward in life.

The first person to forgive is yourself, by taking responsibility for our failures we also have to forgive ourselves for them. There are people in this world who have succeeded in making you fail. With these people, you have to forgive them but you can never forget. By holding on to the stress and the anger these people have caused you, it will only serve to age you and bring you down.

Another reason to consider forgiving others is that some people you may have relied on aren't as responsible as you thought. If you can forgive your parents, friends, or partners for their mistakes, you can let go of that resentment. Forgiving them would help you accept responsibility for your own failures.

More often though, it is the small things in life that irritate us and wear us down. I've heard it said, don't sweat the small stuff and it is all the small stuff. So often we dwell in the past and blow it out of proportion. Imagine someone cut you off in traffic, instead of passing that anger on to them, you can quickly express that anger to yourself and then move on.

The other day, a guy in a van stalled out in front of me at a traffic light. I was in a huge rush to get somewhere, and had errands to run beforehand. Because of that one guy not paying attention and stalling out, I was ten minutes late. If I had held onto that anger towards him, I wouldn't have been able to feel better. Instead, I forgave the whole situation, myself getting angry, included, and forgot it. There was a weight off my shoulders. I still had that 20 second verbal explosion, but I didn't do it at them. In situations like this, my getting upset is a quick catharsis, then I breathe, forgive and let it go.

Sometimes our forgiveness list includes people that are a little more complex to deal with. Consider our parents, and what benefits to forgiving our parents might be there. For one, forgiving our parents frees us up to raise our kids differently and evolve as a planet and a species. When we are living in the past, holding resentments, our vision is directed towards the past. We cannot be visionary when our gaze is on the past.

There are then situations where we have been harmed and abused and it is not appropriate for you to be the bigger person and forgive them. You don't need forgive people who have seriously abused you. But you can forgive them for being who they are, and you can let go of the past's hold on the present. This can help turn your vision toward the future.

When you are in a bad place it is hard to see how that is empowering and how it can help in the long run. Our forgiveness list and our need to take personal responsibility are interwoven. We have to find out how we are responsible and then we can move on to forgiveness for what we were not responsible for.

What this makes me think of in my own life, is that I once made the choice to get into a toxic relationship. I can't blame anyone for that. But I can forgive her for her role in it. I don't want to talk to her but I can give myself back the power from the person that did me wrong. We don't have to do this kind of deep forgiveness to the other person's face. We can do it all within ourselves, and then move on to bigger and better things.

CHAPTER 13

Find a Success

Often we attribute a lot of our success to luck, and fail to see our role in it, and hence our gifts that want to be expressed. You need to understand even if you got lucky, you still had a choice in it. Luck only meets us halfway, as the old saying goes. So take a moment here and examine what you have done in the past and have chalked up to luck. Think about what role you might have had in that success. Surely, it is not nothing? By locating our successes, we begin to locate our gifts. By building on our gifts, we build confidence but more importantly we build a world that we really want to live in. This in so many ways is the secret to happiness.

It starts though by being able to take responsibility when we do something well. By really feeling that and owning that we shift into a creative energy that makes all kinds of things possible. It isn't just labor, or trial and error. Sometimes, we are successful because we are just simply good at a thing. This is worth knowing. In order to know it, we have to really take a look at the past and accept that often what we thought was luck was really our success. This isn't a task to make us more arrogant or make us have inflated egos. If anything, this should be a humbling realization, because it makes us think and feel our gifts which are natural to us.

A story that comes to mind here is my landing a recent job in sales that was a huge promotion for me. My brother got me the introduction, and it would be easy for me to chalk up the job to him. While that introduction definitely helps, hopefully your family wouldn't just refer you to a job because they like you. They refer you to a job because they think you'd be good at the job. You are the one who has to rise to the occasion. It is you that shines through, in the end.

Our success doesn't happen by accident, these things happen because of us. Take the time, take the self care, to look at your life and the good things in it. Really take a minute to contemplate what role you had in making it all happen. Was it a big role? Or was it a small role? More to the point, what was the quality of the role you played and how can you build off of that quality you possess now. Applying our capacity for success to our present life environment is the key to unlocking so much.

Understanding that you have the power in your choices in the success and the failures of your life is the key to taking your life by the horns. All your choices and all the things that happen, they always lead back to you. My current job in sales is as a lead qualification expert. My brother did refer me but I had also done similar jobs for two years. I succeeded here because of me, and me being aided by my brother. This is something we will take up more in the next section.

CHAPTER 14

Gratitude List

The last few sections have focused on forgiveness, taking responsibility for failures, taking responsibility for our successes, thinking about our legacy. At the heart of all of this are mentors, loved ones, friends-- people who provided us with invaluable growth opportunities, reflections, guidance and information. Feeling grateful for these people and events, and what all of it has done, is an energy that propels us forward in life.

A way to tap in to this is to make a gratitude list. This isn't just for pretty sunsets, or your favorite fast food restaurant. This is thinking about the people and events you are grateful for and the ways in which they have helped cast you into the person you want to be. Gratitude is a way to really move well through appreciation and success.

Let me say more about that by turning again to my personal life.

When I was feeling depressed, I often suppressed any good work I was doing. I would chalk up more of my success to other people than to myself. As I mentioned earlier, it is important to accept your role in your success, but it is equally important never to forget the people who assisted that success, that is, in helping us realize what about their help made that success.

This is a rare and hugely beneficial trait to find in another person. This has helped me so much, and this is a trait which really inspires me to help others more too. Without first realizing where I am a success, I can't ever really know that I was successful. But if I take all the credit, I can't recognize how others helped me. I see the ability to form gratitude as filling in a much needed middle ground, when responding to a success in life.

There are three clear ways I can see to respond:

One is the depressed way, a way that I know well in my life. This is where you lose all of your power. In this version of success, there is no gratitude. No gratitude for yourself, and no gratitude for anyone else. If there is any gratitude, it is only toward the person or thing bestowing this opportunity to you. You are at the mercy and the whims of the universe. That my friend is a dangerous place to be. You can't build anything on this approach.

The second way of responding is the arrogant selfish way. In this way, you are only grateful for yourself in your success. For your ability, your gifts, your hard work. You completely ignore all of the people that have helped you. While that might feel good in the short term, in the long run it will come back to bite you. People will remember you not remembering them, even if it is subconscious, and they will choose to distance themselves from you. Ultimately, we need other people, no matter how gifted we are, to ferry our dreams to success. Sure, these other people might only be motivated by money and power, but even still, it will be a much more pleasant experience for everyone if you are congenial and grateful. People will resent you if you take the selfish approach.

Which brings us to the third way, and best way, of responding to success. You are grateful to yourself and to others. You see that you are right where you need to be, you understand what you did to help and what others did too. This is how you become successful gracefully, how you do not compromise your personal life or your integrity in the process of growing into the person you want to be. We have to remember the people who got us where we are, we need to give credit where credit is due, while also patting ourselves on the back for propelling the whole thing along.

CHAPTER 15

Engaging Alternate Ideas

We often don't really know who we are deep down because we are unwilling to seriously engage with alternate viewpoints and ways of seeing the world. We need to know what does and doesn't resonate with us from a genuine place, from an open place - otherwise, every new encounter is being filtered through an old inaccurate system. This is a recipe for remaining stagnant and not growing into the person you are meant to be.

One way to open our mind up to other ways of being in the world is to engage other people's ideas seriously. This is really the best way to learn anything about ourselves. Sure, we have our pre-set ideas and beliefs about what is right and what is wrong, but somewhere along the way we were impressionable to someone. Any true held belief that doesn't come from just being impressionable has to come through critical engagement, and to critically engage with something doesnt mean to criticize it, all it means is to take it seriously and to look for the merits in the other argument, and see how they weigh against the merits in yours.

This process of measuring is ultimately a process of measuring ourselves - our philosophy and our conscience. This is necessary for making any kind of worldview that isn't just based on bias and opinion. I don't know what kind of person you want to be, but I know that I want to be a person who has a worldview based on an open mind and a critical eye.

Another important piece that comes through engaging alternate ideas is that through this we learn how to accept others who have different ideas than ours. This is a huge benefit to whatever our mission is, because this is a great way to solve a lot of the issues that we see today. People tend to live under the predisposed idea that if something someone says threatens their belief then it threatens them personally. If we just think about that for a second, we can see that it is not true. The way we change the world is through conversation. If you can't have a conversation with someone different than you because you are so caught up in your own opinion, you have no chance of changing the world.

The alternative is a beautiful one. What if we tried to learn more about each other and spend more time together in that process of learning? Then it wouldn't be so scary to be open to someone else's point of view. Once you can visualize their point of view, you can actually talk to them, rather than just talking at them.

Just the other day, I was having a conversation with someone and we were on very different sides of a political question. I was able to say to them, "I totally understand what you are saying and I am not saying you are wrong, but can you engage with my point?" They couldn't. They responded to that with another tirade of why they were right. What I was really asking was, "Can you break out of your own mindset to see what I am saying?" That fact that they couldn't, got on my nerves so much. I would hate to know that I go through the world doing the same thing with the same closed mindset, so I take steps to be conscious that I don't. I take time to consider someone else's point of view before responding to it.

You might get accused of being spineless, or lacking integrity, but the truth is far from that. In reality, you are acting with the most integrity, and a more flexible approach often means more strength in communicating what you really do think.

How can we know the person we want to become when we can't even open ourselves up to other potentials and other possibilities? The simple answer is, we can't. We need to be able to see ourselves clearly becoming the person we want to be.

When you make a part of that new person, someone who is open to taking other ideas seriously and engaging thoughts that may seem foreign, it is like putting another carburetor on your engine. It should rev you up and excite you to get to consider other possibilities.

What if you had never changed your mind about anything, what kind of person would you be? It is essential to do what it takes to become bigger, and that often starts with taking other people's thoughts and feelings seriously.

Even if you know you will disagree with the other person, you can learn something about them and about yourself by listening deeply and closely. It makes it much more possible to become the person you want to be when you are able to get to know others in a respectful and complex way.

CHAPTER 16

Today is a Good Day

By even imagining that today is special, it magically becomes special. Our minds are powerful things, but if we are able to harness and train them for all they are worth, we can truly transform our realities. How we feel about our day-to-day and the energy we bring into our day-to-day profoundly affects what we are doing. There can't be any great strides in our life if we are living in a state of anxiety and depression.

There is an ongoing debate in the depression and anxiety community about the best way to treat what can be a crippling illness. I have never been clinically depressed, but I have had episodes of acute depression, and when I have been depressed, people without depression will always tell me to "just be happy". When someone is saying that, it can feel really bad. What do they know about my life? I want to ask them. The truth is, if you tell yourself something enough times, you will be reinforcing it, and slowly over time it will build into a new reality. The experts call this positive psychology, and it has been proven to work. You can start by pretending you have a secret no one else knows about. A really good one - like it is Christmas, or like you are holding a winning lottery ticket. These sorts of positive thought processes can radically transform our lives.

We have to tell ourselves that today is a good day, today is special, because it is all true. The more you do that, the more you can face bad things with an attitude of, "it's ok, I just have to get through it". One of the key points of this section is that when you have something good going on, when you are telling yourself positive things, it is good to keep it to yourself, and not to let others get you down. When we share this with the wrong people, we invite their negativity.

I have gone through my battle with depression and negative thoughts. What got me through it was a consistent push of "I will be ok". This became for me a continuous internal monologue. There wasn't one specific moment where the depression lifted. It really was more of a gradual thing - if you do it every day, that is, tell yourself that this is a special day and you have a special place in it, the more you won't have to do this over the long term. If you do it once a day for a long enough time, you will find that your life has shifted around you.

Now if I have a bad day, I just tell myself I have to go to bed and tomorrow will be a good day.

It is amazing that it has taken me such a long time to realize something that is this simple.It is not a specific one time thing, this is not a quick fix, you have to tell yourself you are happy for six months, and the goal is to think it, believe, act it, and then eventually you will feel and understand it. This will take you from living as if it is just another day you have to sludge through, and into living in a world that is special, and that you are a special part of. We have to retrain our minds to be able to see this.

CHAPTER 17

Learn to Say Yes and No

By acknowledging our innermost life path we are able to say yes and no from a place of our soul, our deepest desires, drives and instincts. It is funny thinking that we have to learn how to say yes and say no. Those are two of the first words we learn as babies. And no more two words are essential in shaping our life path. Of course, we think of big moments where yes and no have clear impact. The famous wedding "I do" to the signing of a business deal. In fact, we pay more attention to the yeses in our lives, and less attention to the nos.

The nos have just as much, if not more, impact in shaping our worlds.

When we are able to freely say yes and no to the world we open up to ourselves. We are able to know ourselves well enough to say, "that is for me, that is not for me". This takes a lot of trust in ourselves and the ability to endure what might be negative pushback or conflict when we do say no. But since it is in the best interest of our lives, it becomes easier to say no as a clear and simple statement of preference. We are no longer bogged down in the details of going "what will they think, how will they respond to this, what if they don't like me". As we develop a more solid relationship with ourselves, it becomes easier to say yes and no. In fact, we find that being able to confidently say yes and no to things is a sign that we are becoming the person that we want to be. Of course, we have to negotiate with others and say yes when we'd otherwise say no, and say no when we'd otherwise say yes. We all live in some kind of a community.

In negotiating to cohabitate well with other people, we are always on a deeper level saying yes to being in a world surrounded by this person we might be compromising for, and saying no to being all on our own. This too can become a conscious decision aimed at us being the person we'd like to become, rather than a sheepish reaction to just going along with whatever is comfortable.

So how can we begin to get to a place in our lives where we are able to confidently say both yes and no? It is helpful to connect with something really deep and in your nature, and to make decisions from that place. It is also important to tap into that place to console you if you have to say no to something you were really looking forward to, or have to say yes to doing something for a family member or friend that isn't the most fun.

Before I found this place in myself, I would always have a hard time saying no to people. I didn't really know what I wanted, so I just went along with whatever. This chipped away at my integrity and the way my life unfolded. Once I reclaimed my own lodestar, my guiding light, I was able to just listen and not react to what other people would present me with. Everything was an opportunity.

Parents giving suggestions in the past would infuriate me. Now, some of suggestions I like, some I don't. My grandparents always said I should be a lawyer. It was hard to say no because I really didn't really know what I wanted, so I wound up disappointing them, giving them a false expectation. They would have loved and supported me no matter what, especially if I really knew myself and what I wanted in life. Knowing what you want and understanding yourself deep down lets you guide yourself from a place that is secure. What you are working towards you can hold already. You don't necessarily need to be able to share what you want or even say it. You need to know what feels good to you in an authentic way, and that will make it so that you are more secure in your choices. I am able to say no and that makes everything a yes. Everything is a yes to myself: saying no is saying yes to who you want to be.

CHAPTER 18

Express a Need

When we get to know ourselves, and start really becoming the person we are, we start to get to know what our needs are. For most of us, those needs involve other people. We might have the need for something basic, like love and interesting friendships. Or, it might be more specific, we might have a need for a good head scratch, as nothing else calms us down quite like that. Simply put, human beings are human animals, and we have very basic needs. We oftentimes remain locked in place and locked in our own trauma and self neglect because we don't ask for help or for what we need. It can be as simple as asking for a hug.

There is nothing embarrassing about asking for what you need when you know what you need is coming from the secure sense of self you cherish-- when it is coming from the person you want to become.

I lived a lot of my life not being able to express what I really want. I was always ok with the situation around me with the people I love. I was happy for what I got, but a lot of my needs went unmet. This is not because those around me weren't willing to meet them. It is because they simply just didn't know what they were. How could they help meet my needs when I was unable to express those needs. It is pretty easy when we are babies, but as we get older and we learn more about the people we want to be, our needs become more nuanced, more complex. I never said anything to those around me only because I didn't want to disturb or upset them, but this harmed my life. To be the fullest expression of ourselves, we need our needs to be met.

By truly understanding yourself, it becomes much easier to express those needs that will make your life better. A hug, help with a paper, a meal. You can look inside and find out what you need.

A key to making this work is to be able to express what you need without expecting anything in return, and to always feel good because you are always looking out for yourself, regardless of what the response from the other person is.

A big area for me, where asking for needs often comes up, is in relationships. In the past, I couldn't express what I needed because I'd be insulted or humiliated. Yes, I was in many toxic relationships. I've grown to be able to express what I need without fear and get the dopamine boost that comes from having your needs met. Especially in dating, knowing who I am and what I need to express guides me toward who I need around me. Before I found out how to say yes or no, before I really knew the person I wanted to become, I always wanted to surround myself with anyone willing to surround themselves with me. That was a pretty low bar. That all changed once I knew I had needs and that people who couldn't respond to them wouldn't be able to help me grow and move forward.

All of this goes back to knowing yourself, knowing that you have needs, and then it is easy to not surround yourself with people that can't give you what you need.

CHAPTER 19

Ask Someone What They Need

We just talked about how hard it is to ask for what we need. If we put ourselves in someone else's shoe, they are also going through the same thing. Isn't that amazing? What can we do for someone else. Well, we can write a book, we can tell them about how much better their lives would be if they did ask for what they needed, or, we could ask them what they need. Though the other person may not be vulnerable enough to tell you the truth or the heart of it, you are at the very least opening up a door for them. For a second, they will feel the relief of how good it feels to be able to ask for what they need and to have those needs met. As we discover who we are and the person we want to become, it gradually becomes easier to both ask for what we need and to ask others for what they need. The two go hand in hand. In fact, we often miss opportunities to become ourselves because we aren't vulnerable enough to offer ourselves to others. It is a two way street.

Earlier in the book I talked about a huge door that was opened for me by simply asking a stranger what they needed. We can do this with loved ones or with perfect strangers. It is ultimately just a way of being in the world, and a way of being that makes us more likely to fall into good and fruitful situations. Another benefit of asking others what they need is we gradually begin to see what it is that we have to give. This is a hugely beneficial insight when we are doing the work of becoming the person we want to be. We really learn about ourselves in giving ourselves to others. For me, something I have learned is that I always want to be involved and want to have a lot of experiences in the world. Getting involved and putting myself out there applies to all areas of life: sports, work, school, and chores. That is a quality about me that is really a gift, essential to the person I want to become, and made visible by asking others what they need.

Not asking people what they need is a really foreign idea to me. The majority of progression in my life has come from asking others what they need. This is not about being a kiss ass, this is about wanting genuinely to apply my best self to the world. Asking a boss what exactly they need out of a role is not for their sake, but for my sake. Then I can over-exceed it and be that person that I want to be.

It doesn't seem like a good idea not to ask other people what they need, I think you probably wouldn't be doing something you like if you approach life that way, because you won't be giving your best self to the world. People who don't ask what others need end up getting told what to do. Getting told what to do is a lot less fun than asking someone what they need. Also, since all humans have similar needs, in asking others what they need you get to learn more about what you might need. You can approach asking others as really asking yourself.

When I was having trouble at a job, I asked myself what I needed to get better and feel better, that was the same as asking my boss what they needed. You can be that someone you ask, too.

CHAPTER 20

The Impossible List

Often we hold ourselves back by saying we can't do it. Of course we can't do it when we say we can't. The funny thing is, a lot of what we say we can't do, we actually can do. I thought making my bed was impossible, clearly that is possible. Even if I only do it two or three times a week, that is still a huge leap above what I was doing before - nada. The truth is, we hold ourselves back with our internal lists of what can and cannot be done. Nothing is impossible. Think about it like this: historically, as a human species, everything was impossible, until we did it. Think about going to the moon, having a computer in your hand, having classes online, everything was impossible, all of this was the stuff of the impossible list. That is, except for those that have no impossible list.

Even something like traveling across continents in a matter of hours, something we take totally for granted, this was the kind of visionary thinking. Push your limits. Start with little things. This kind of breakthrough starts with something like making your bed, and it ends with your dream job. I never thought I'd make my bed three times a week. I certainly never thought I'd quit my job. I couldn't even have pictured myself going on a camping trip.

Jumping off a cliff? Forget about it. But the truth is, the more you do the more you feel you can do, and that builds into a meaningful and rewarding future.

So why do you think we keep things on our impossible list? Think about it. How does it benefit us to do that? It benefits us in a few ways, but on closer examination, it definitely isn't supporting the kind of person we want to become. We keep things on that list because it makes us feel in control, it makes us feel safe. We tell ourselves we know our limits. But isn't that just another way of saying we are afraid of failure? What is failure when we fail in support of something we love and cherish, or in other words, the person we want to become.

The failures, as we have discussed, allow us to grow into ourselves. But more to the point, starting to remove things from the impossible list doesn't have to be scary, because we can do it slowly over time, and start with things that really are in our control.

Applying for jobs that you'd find more interesting, that is something in your control.

Making your bed, that is something in your control. Really, everything in this book is somehow in your control. When we take small steps and build on them, we are able to ultimately live life without an impossible list. We replace it with a curious attitude about ourselves and the people we could become and the impact we can have on the world. Sounds good, right?

CHAPTER 21

Change Up Your Look

How we look says a lot about who we are. It is the first impression we give other people in our day, but more importantly, it is the first impression we give ourselves in the morning. Consider if you have fallen into a rhythm of simplicity around your personal style and what it means to you. Do you feel comfortable in your own skin, like you have really landed on something? Or do you feel like something maybe could change and free up a whole new possibility of who you could be and the person you could become. Changing up our look - our clothes, a haircut, even the way we carry yourself - what an easy way to change who we are and get a sense of the way you are experienced in the world. Changing up your style is a good way to change up your mindset.

Think about the old and awful trope about how people that dye their hair must have some insecurity issues. More likely than that, they are just changing up their look to find out who they are.

It takes that kind of boldness to find who you are. There is nothing wrong with that, we stigmatize it because we ourselves are afraid of taking the same leap.

I was like this in high school, I literally had no style. Most of this was because I lived in the smallest of towns, but a good deal of it had to do with my fear of taking a risk and mixing up my look. Thanks to my sister Megan, I came to see the appeal of looking nice. I experimented with other outfits, and it turned out that I really have two modes: a full suit (or at least a button down and tie) or sweatpants. I can still wear sweatpants and slippers and make it true to me, they can look nice and match colors.

I was always comfortable in my own skin which is why I could wear a onesie to school. Even though I look casual I looked good, because I was being true to me. Some kids might have laughed at me for not ascribing to the latest high school fashion, but often those were the very same kids who didn't have a sense of themselves.

As my life progressed, and people around me started wanting to find themselves, they started to take more notice of my style. By switching up my look a little bit and focusing on how I was going to dress and how I presented, I started to get more compliments and in turn started gaining more confidence.

There was a journey to get to the comfort of living in my own style. Looking good makes you feel good. Don't be afraid to mix it up. Even when I was in young, sometimes I would wear a button down and tie, just to switch it up and see how I feel.

In general, people don't dress super nice, and it can be to their own detriment. I used to wear a suit most days to a job I had. People would ask me, "why do you wear a suit, when you work the phone?" My response was always that I look good, I feel good, I do well. I liked to imagine that the client can feel that the person on the other end of the phone is wearing a suit. It shows in my confidence, I liked to think that it shines through to the other end of the line. I am the most outgoing and confident when I feel at my best, finding your style by switching up your look is a major step to find what makes you most comfy in your own skin. Let go of what you've been told to wear and find out what the you that you want to become wears.

CHAPTER 22

Open Your Mind

Here is the truth: there are lessons in everything. Every day that passes is full of lessons. We accumulate wisdom, the ability to choose right over wrong and make good decisions, by paying close mind to the lessons available in our life. One trick to getting ahead and to becoming the person that you want to be is to have a hunger for lessons. There are plenty of obvious lessons we encounter. Little kids learn that the stove is hot by touching it, eventually they will give in to curiosity no matter what their parents have said. Lo and behold, their parents were right. This is why we can't just rely on books, on mentors or on family members to give us our life lessons. We have to get them from the world directly.

The surest way to this is to simply open our minds and always wanting to keep that open mind. Sure, it helps to have mentors and people you can reflect on your life lessons with. These kinds of relationships are indispensable and will come up later in the book. But there are lessons in everything. Even if you don't have a mentor, you can be your own mentor and learn from life, and you can be your own friend to reflect with. This creates a very dynamic experience of life that keeps life interesting and fresh for years to come. You trust that life can guide you where you need to go if you pay attention to the lessons and keep an open mind about yourself and the person you want to become. You learn a lot about people, yourself, and the world because lessons are found in a lot of places and those become places you grow.

Earlier in the book, I mentioned some trouble I got into in high school. I had to go to a drug court program for a very minor offense, and in a situation that was stupid at best. Some of the other kids in that program were different from me, they wouldn't sit back and learn and take in the lessons they were being given. Instead, they would sit back and resist and be close minded. They didn't want to be there and it showed. I also didn't want to be there, but I shut up and went through the program and I learned a lot about other people and also about myself. The key to all of this was to stay very open minded and to open myself up to the experience at hand.

Rather than getting angry at the experience, I tried to look and see what lessons were available for me in it. Even the most open minded people have those times where they are closed off to something, and usually this is when it gets uncomfortable.

Whenever something seems bad, it is good to have that second thought of asking yourself, "am I just closed off to this?" A closed mind will never grow, and quite possibly you are closed off to the opportunity in the difficult experience. If you get all of your wisdom in life from a closed mind, you are really just reinforcing what you already know. The lessons you learn only come from the scope of your own life as you know it. This isn't fair or wise, and it isn't going to push you toward becoming the person you want to be.

CHAPTER 23

Fear List

We all live with fears. Some people fear what tomorrow will bring. Others are haunted by the fears of yesterday. We all have fears today. Our fears are often subconscious. We don't even become aware of them unless we pay close and careful attention to the things that we avoid. Do you avoid having a long term relationship? Maybe you are afraid of intimacy. Do you avoid going out for long walks by yourself, maybe you fear the crime in your neighborhood.

Some of our fears are genuinely external and rational, but most of our fears are internal and the subject of our own habits and our own self-talk – what we tell ourselves about the world that we live in. There is an old saying that goes, "know your enemy, and your enemy is yourself." The key to beating our enemy is to know our enemy. We must come to know ourselves. This is what separates the greater minds out from those that just go along with their unconscious habits and activities.

If we pause and consider that our enemies and our fears aren't external, but rather that they are internal thought habits, built up and reinforced by our experiences of the world, the question then becomes how to overcome them, how to change them. We can accept that we have fears, we can know and understand them. Changing them though also requires seeing how they aren't true.

Usually, the way that we prove they aren't true is by taking the risk to prove it, we have to live it out in our experience. This sort of leap is what distinguishes this kind of conquering of fear as courageous and heroic work. We tell ourselves that we want to live the best life possible, and we understand that to get there we have to overcome the fears that are holding us back.

So go ahead and make a list of your fears, and then start taking steps to cross them off.

To get to where you want to go, you are going to have to overcome some fears.

When you look at your fear list, you will probably notice that there aren't a lot of other people on it. It is very high schoolish to have thoughts like "he is my enemy". As we mature, we grow out of viewing the world that way. People no longer stand in for what usually is a much deeper fear. We are forced to begin to confront our fears, and hopefully to work through them.

For me, one of my major fears is about how my ideas will be received. One way of working through that is to take the risk of writing this book. Now that I have begun to conquer that fear, new fears have emerged. I have fear of backlash, controversy after I finish this book. Conversely, I have a fear of success. Believe it or not, I have a fear of making it really work. I have a fear that once I make it work, I will lose it. The only way to work through these fears us to be really honest with myself about them. But the truth is,

I would rather be where I want to be for a week and fail rather than never get there because of fear of failing.

So take your fears and write them out so you know them and understand them. You may never overcome all of them, and that is ok, we can learn to live well with our fears. Some of them may even come true. But you can never please everybody, so why not please yourself by pushing through fear. You can find your comfort zone by finding your fears, because through knowing your fears, you know your greatest enemy. Once you have clarity on that, you have freedom to control them, rather than be controlled by them.

CHAPTER 24

Know Your Strengths

People stick around us because they get something out of us being in their lives. This is obvious. Even if it is the smallest reason, there are good things about all of us that make people want to be around.

How often do you sit back and think about what it must be that you bring into the lives of others to make them want to have you around. There are others that depend on you for some kind of support and community. Maybe it is your intelligence, maybe it is your humor or empathy. Maybe it is a particular skill set they have not mastered. Finding out what it is can allow us to get to know our natural strengths. Once we know our natural strengths, we can build on our natural strengths and turn them into the fullest expressions of what they are.

Instead of shooting in the dark and wondering what your strengths could be, and what it is that you bring into the lives of those around you, especially your friends, you can just ask them.

Go ahead and think about someone who is in your support network. Because they care about you, you should be able to ask them what your strengths are. I hope that the people you consider friends, the people in your support network, are people who are able to push you and respect you and admire you. If they aren't then you have a different problem on your hands. You might want to look at the earlier chapters that have to do with really locating the person that you want to become. Once you feel that you have people in your life you can ask, just ask them. What do I do to make you want to be around me? Contemplate the answer and see if there are any strengths in there that you can apply to other areas of your life.

Now, of course you could say that no one is in your life for a reason and approach this chapter with a depressed attitude. You would probably find out that it is not true by just opening yourself up to the people around you. It can be hard to swallow the truth that we are appreciated by other people. Perhaps certain individuals in our lives have left us to feel otherwise. One person's actions and opinion about you may be so far from the truth.

The purpose of this experiment is to find out what you are good and bad at and build on what's good. We can be good at anything if we put enough time and concentration in, but building on our natural talents is really the key to success.

I think about myself. I could be good at a lot, but I am finding things that I truly enjoy, so I am going to build on those things like business, visionary thinking, and branding.

There may be people in your life that you respect and love - build on that - there is probably

something about them that you could also see in yourself. The trick to getting going on all of this is in being ok with what you don't do well. Then you get to the joy of things. I take pleasure in what I do well, and I find people to work with that know how to do what I can't do well.

There is a story about a plumber, an electrician , and a suburban dad. The suburban dad sees a really bad clogged toilet and tries to fix it himself, wanting to prove how handy he is. The suburban dad makes the situation much worse, and has to call the plumber. His bill is $250. An electrician sees the same clogged toilet, and he knows what it means to be an expert in something. He thinks, I could probably fix it, but I should just let the expert do it. His plumber bill is $100.

Do you want to show off your ego or do you want to be able to admit you aren't good at something? To be able to admit that you have to have the inner confidence that you are good at other things. When you find out what you are good at and enjoy doing, you can use that to cope with and get over things that you are bad at. This all starts with finding out what your strengths are. The best way to start doing that is to ask others who know you well.

CHAPTER 25

Admit What You Really Want

We go through life hiding from ourselves. We hide from what we really want and feel we deserve. It would just be too good to be true if everything we wanted came to fruition. Or we tell ourselves that if it all did come true, we definitely would lose it. When you read this here, it sounds ridiculous, doesn't it?

We settle for second best because we don't admit that we deserve first best, but in order to admit that we deserve first best, we need to develop a solid relationship with the person we want to become and we need to take solid, concrete steps to realize that vision. Our life is flashing before our eyes. We go through it in the comfort of second best, but then a day comes where we know deep down that we could and should do better. We should seek more. We should reach out to the person we want to be. We should seek ourselves, but instead we stay guarded to the world and to others.

How do you not settle for second best? It starts by finding what you want your goal to be and not losing track of it. My goal was to create a movement that would be influential. I really need to say my goal is this because goals are living things, even once we reach them, they morph and change into a similar version of what they were before. My plan has changed a lot, but I haven't lost sight of my end goal. My plan has changed because we have to adapt to our environments. However, we have to always stay connected to our inner self. One way to maintain this connection through changing tides is to make a plan.

Let's talk more about goals. There are two main kinds of goals, there are goals that have a quality to them, rather than a specific thing. For instance, a goal of "being in love" is a quality. A goal of being in love with a famous person is a specific thing. Sometimes we have to admit that there are many steps towards our goals, and making smaller goals can aid in the process of mapping our growth. And sometimes, those steps turn out to be the goal itself in a different form.

Say you really want your dream job. Then you get a new job that you don't think is that dream job, but two months into it you realize it is about as good as any job will ever get.

The flip side of that is when we set out toward our goals and don't want to settle for less than the best, but end up doing a lot of what we think we want, and along the way often end up learning a lot of these things are things that we really don't want to do. Having an end goal and a plan while remaining open to trying and doing other things is the key toward really ending up in a sweet place.

There are no bad goals. Whatever your goal is, being a good parent, an activist, even just trying to be the best you is all centered around having a goal and having a plan. Try to think about it in terms that are more than trying to weigh the pros and cons of what it is you want, try to think about the steps that will get you there.

Remember, what you want doesn't have to be anything too specific. It can be anything you want, so long as you have that end goal and you aren't willing to settle for second best.

By being able to admit that I am not at the best version of what I want yet, and see that I am taking steps to get there, makes me less likely to settle for something that is not as good as it could otherwise be if I saw all of my goals through.

CHAPTER 26

Find Great Minds

By looking to great minds of the past and present, we realize that we are not alone in our struggle to get bigger and to be influential .We need to invite them, their wisdom and their ideas, deeper into our lives. By doing that we open the doorway to being moved to take bolder and more innovative action within our own lives. We often forget that the humans of the past, from the person who invented the wheel to someone like Leonardo DaVinci, Marie Curie, or Georgia O'Keeffe, all existed within the same net of human struggles, difficulties, and ultimately, opportunities.

By studying the great minds of the past and people who come from similar backgrounds as ourselves, we can begin to learn how people respond to life situations and become successful. We can see what is there for us to incorporate into our own life. Most importantly, we can see the motives that drove these greater minds to accomplish what they did. Usually, two clear themes emerge, curiosity and the urge to be influential.

When I think of a greater mind, I think of someone like Barack Obama. Regardless of what you think about his politics, he has a certain presence that is the vehicle for his influence. He is calm, cool and collected, and this makes him influential. People listen and respond to him. This will set him apart from others in the history books. I also look to Abraham Lincoln as an inspiration. It is not because he was always honest, we all know that he wasn't. He was great at politics. He had clear goals of leadership, and when it came to the Civil War, he knew how to fight the battle that he needed to fight.

He was able to use his natural edge toward leadership and influence, and he accomplished one of the most consequential changes in the history of the United States. Whether he was a good person is subjective, what is objective is what he got done. We can learn from that way of looking at things. People of the past are remembered by their works. That is what shines though, and what we must always keep at the center of our mind.

When you look at the great minds of the past, many people see them only as role models. If you dig a little deeper and look at what is really there, for instance when you look at where they were when they were your age, you see many were right where you are now.

Perhaps they are even farther from their goals when they were where you are. We can't let the great minds of our time make us feel inhibited. They need to inspire us. We need to feel that we are an important part of conversation with them. Whether it is a politician, and artist, a physicist or architect, a businessman, you are connected to them through history. Because of that, you can learn from their successes and failures. You in fact are at an advantage. Have gratitude for the people who have gone before you.

In my story, I am drawn to people who used their influence to effect change in the lives of those who needed it most. Someone like LeBron James could just sit on his laurels, but he does much behind the scenes to help those in his native city of Cleveland and beyond feel empowered, inspired, and not have to live in a struggle for basic needs.

It is best when you are looking to the past to find the people that align with your message. Remember to maintain an open mind. A lot of time people do align with your mission, they just speak differently. Invite their life and their experience into your life and grow from it, that way you can learn a lot from their success and failures. Most importantly, you can feel part of something bigger than yourself. When we take what has already been created and grow it further, we exercise influence in the universe.

CHAPTER 27

Your Charity Work

It is important to do charity work in this life. This isn't to just show off, or because it is something you think you should do. We do charity work ultimately to learn more about ourselves. Not only do we get to feel more acutely the advantages we have going into this life. We also get the pleasure of experiencing other people having their lives changed. Let's begin by considering why it is important to do charity work. It is important for so many reasons, I will only be able to touch on a few.

In essence, anyone who has the ability to think about charity work is someone who is lucky enough to do that kind of thinking. Perhaps we were raised to think that way, that is a sign of having good and nurturing parents. Perhaps we have surplus wealth, that is a sign of material abundance. I suppose there is one situation in which luck does not play into it, in the case where your own open mind has led you to consider the merits of doing charity work. To me, the largest benefit of charity work is that through giving to others selflessly you learn more about the problems you want to solve. You can look for where it feels natural for you to give to others.

Everyone has something that deep down they want to address in this world. I have met people that on first contact seem morose, like they have some axe to grind with humanity. These are people you might even call apathetic. Whenever you start to talk to someone like that, you quickly find out that they still have something that they want to do to make the world a better place. We all have that calling. When we stop to think about this, it just goes to show you who you are deep down. You are an altruistic and caring person.

I find, ironically, that some of the people that act like they care a lot and are in fact not very charitable at all. Then there are others who act like they don't care at all and are very giving. Go figure.

When I look at a lot of the chapters in my life I see my desire to do charitable works within them. For instance, proceeds from this book will be donated to education reform groups. That is because I see the mission of this book and my desire for influence through it as inextricable from the wider project of education reform. That wider project is a project that requires charitable activity. It could also be something a little stranger, a desire to change the world for good.

Everything that is going to make me money, that extra profit isn't just going to go into my hedge fund position, it is going to go into me trying to have the most influence on the world that I possibly can have. That is my deepest goal, not just to make money so I am perceived to be a successful entrepreneur. Charity is what gives me the most meaning.

It feels good to be connected to our fellow human beings, and that is not a bad thing.

Feeling good in giving to others doesn't discount the value of what you are doing, if anything it adds value to it. It feels really good to give and to structure your goals around some kind of charitable mission.

CHAPTER 28

Make Yourself Accountable

It is so important to make sure that we are accountable to our own dreams, visions, and desires. It is too easy in this life to just keep things locked in our own minds. What good does that do, ultimately? We can amuse ourselves by thinking or feeling that we can do something that stretches our limits, but unless we set up a system of accountability, it can easily just be our imagination running away with us. That won't produce the real tactile results that we want in this world. So what are some important first steps that we can take toward making this happen? There are the obvious ones we've already gone through that involve making lists, making plans, gathering information and inspiration, working on our fears. But there is something much simpler and ready for you to do, that might seem scary at first, but will pay off big in the end.

By telling someone else about your goals and your plans, you all of a sudden up the stakes of what you are doing. When we keep things to ourselves, we don't become responsible to others. Though our goals are our own, and it is easy to think that we aren't responsible to anyone but ourselves in realizing them, the truth is that plenty of other people will enjoy the fruits of you realizing your goals.

If you are an architect, and your goal is to design one of the most beautiful 21st century office buildings, it is ultimately other people that will be enjoying your goal once it is realized. And these are people that will enjoy it every day. We have to consider other people when we consider our goals, and by sharing them with someone, we make ourselves responsible to that person in realizing them. Not to mention the practicality of having people there to get you moving and keep you on track, when life inevitably throws us curve balls and we veer off track. We have to be responsible to others to be successful. If you don't tell anyone, you can keep yourself less accountable. Look and see if that is the reason you aren't telling others about your goals.

That said, one of the worst things we can do is to tell a negative person about your goals. People can get nasty, jealous, or just try and talk us down. You want positive energy and support, but you also want to keep yourself accountable to others. So it is important to only share these things with people you know would love to see you succeed. The way to know that is mostly just a feeling. We can tell in our guts when we are around someone who wouldn't be happy for our success. And just remember, that is probably someone who is pretty far away from their own success story. Because as we know, once we get launched on our success stories, the successes of others around us only offer fuel to our fire. And the failures too, as we join a community of people trying to become their best self.

As soon as you start talking about something, it instantly becomes more real, and the thoughts behind it become more real. This is one of the secrets and mysteries of the universe. So don't be afraid to talk about it if it is your dream. Do what you need to do in yourself to get to a point where you are comfortable enough to talk about it. This might mean conquering your fears, trusting yourself, or trusting that others will still support you if you fail and that they want to see you succeed. But the truth is, if no one else knows about your plan, you probably will give up on it. We have to put it in the world for the world to give it back to us.

CHAPTER 29

Take That First Step

We often dream of things but never actually take the first simple step to making it a reality. Our hopes, dreams and goals all live within our minds. You have to take concrete action to make those a reality outside of yourself. Without taking a first step, things will always live in the realm of the possible, not the realm of the known and the seen. How can you avoid that? People can't enjoy your ideas as much as they can enjoy what your ideas produce. We have to connect ourselves to a reality that is bigger than just us and take those first steps to break out of the box.

Figuring out who you want to become will take a lot of failure. And one of the best ways to fail is by taking a first step. Often, after we've taken a first step, we look back and think taking the first step really wasn't that hard. It is the space before taking that first step which presents us with so much trouble and heaviness. The best way to break out of that inertia is to use whatever you have to make things known to the world, usually your words and your hands. So take your fingers and go ahead and Google what you need to get where you want to go.

Maybe it is medical school, you can research what you need to get there, and then you can take your pen and journal (essential tools for the work of becoming the person we want to be). Whatever it is, you can take some first steps to make it so. Maybe your goal is to be a good parent, you can try and get a job around kids, or you can order a parenting book online, or even just listen to a podcast on your way to work. Taking that first step is crucial for putting everything into perspective.

There is a pain and torture of working through learning, but when we have a clear goal in mind, things have a funny way of getting easy. Taking the first steps will either motivate you to take more, different first steps, or to continue on the path you are on. One question I get a lot is the question which asks, "How will I know it is the right first step for me to take?" Well, getting to know the person you want to become will certainly help with that. I took a lot of first steps and didn't know which ones to follow up on. However, I always knew when it was the right first step to build on if I found myself always coming back to it.

You might make a list of the steps you need to take to achieve your dreams, and then a week later think about something on that list that you want to research more. The process of building on the right first step is really natural and the pain of the initial effort will quickly turn into the joy of building the life you want and becoming the person you want to be. You may not know which first step you want to cultivate until you keep taking first steps and then come back to something, so there is no harm in just taking that first step. If it doesn't stick, so what, something else will - especially if you take the other lessons in this book to heart.

What is your first step going to be? Try and take one today. All you need to do is look around and consider the world you are living in. There is always a first step five feet away. The trick is to just move things from only existing in your mind to also existing in the world. So if you, for instance, are busy and think to yourself, "I will do my first step later," you can instead take a step by writing down a note that is a self-reminder. We have to anchor our dreams in the world to have a stable foundation on which to develop.

CHAPTER 30

Set Sail

By living the stories you want others to tell about you, you begin to construct your reality in a way that will create a legacy that is bigger than you could ever imagine. Rather than living in someone else's world, you begin to make something that can hold YOU.

We need to, through our life, create a vessel through which ourselves can be expressed. By doing this, we create a legacy. Through this, we become interesting old people. We want to be making the stories now to tell our grandchildren. By keeping that in mind, we will quickly land our eyes on what it is we really need to be doing and working on. We can become part of something bigger than ourselves by thinking about family and thinking about how time passes in this kind of a way. We have to take bold actions now to be remembered later, and to help carve a path that others might benefit from. This is what it means to live a meaningful life.

I had a lot of fear about having a book. I really worried about how people would respond. One of my most recurring thoughts was whether or not I will get ridiculed. Even more intense than that, I thought, will I get hated? People will show up to read this book with all kinds of preconceived notions and ideals about what they will get out of it. Hopefully, people like yourself get a lot out of it. But I wrote it with a bigger and more expansive picture in mind. I wrote this book as a major step in becoming the person I want to be, the person I want my grandchildren to know. In order for me to get there, I had to begin. I had to take concrete steps toward making it so. I went beyond any fear or hate or praise or negativity. I moved past what I wanted in terms of short term gratification, and thought that if in forty years this book can have some kind of positive impact I did my job.

Ultimately, when we think in terms of becoming the person we want the future generations to know, it is deeply empowering. This thought becomes an event when we take some kind of action to concretize it. Whether it is telling your kids or writing it down or making a piece of art or a poem or a lesson, or even just trying to make a difference or make a change, we can do actual things in our lives that have massive ripples outward through time. For me, the overall goal is not having a fear of getting my message across. This book is an example of that.

People might ask me, how did you write this you're not a writer? I have a good answer for them, and for the future generations that will know me as a father, a grandfather, and hopefully an innovative entrepreneur. I can tell them that I am a designer and a visionary thinker, so I compiled a team, something I know how to do, to make this book a reality so that I could pass these rules for my life down.

Once you care enough about the message behind something, you don't care about the negative feedback you might get in making it a reality. By locating this drive in you, you have found something intrinsically successful enough to push through the negative feedback you will inevitably encounter on your road to realization, on your road to becoming the person you want to become.

Lightning Source UK Ltd.
Milton Keynes UK
UKHW020804291221
396330UK00012B/860